ocean sur

una nueva editorial latinoamericana

COLOUR PHOTOGRAPHY

COLOUR PHOTOGRAPHY

Michael Busselle

Octopus Books

ACKNOWLEDGEMENTS

Special photography: Michael
Busselle.

Cover Photography:
Robert Harding Picture Library
front cover above right, Carol Jopp
back cover left, H Ross front cover
below right; Colin Molyneux front
cover left, back cover right.

First published in one volume 1985

This edition first published in 1988
by Octopus Books Limited,
Michelin House, 81 Fulham Road,
London SW3 6RB

ISBN 0 7064 1897 2

Printed in Hong Kong

CONTENTS

INTRODUCTION

Although the vast majority of photographs taken today are in colour, it is a sad fact that few of them produce really pleasing pictures. Far too often the photographer has concentrated on the subject, depth of field and focussing, without realising that a confusion of clashing colours will ruin the eventual effect.

Avoiding this all too common fault involves learning how to handle the relationship between colours and how to choose and frame a picture to achieve a harmonious whole, in which the colours make the picture rather than detract from it. Once at ease with this, you will probably want to experiment with filters to create your own colour effects – for example, enhancing the blue of a Mediterranean sky, or increasing the dramatic effect of a thundercloud.

This book explains the different sorts of filter, the types of colour film and using colour to express mood. It tells you how to restrict colour range to make your shots more effective, how to use multiple exposure and how to make a 'slide sandwich' to combine two transparencies to form one image. You will discover how best to photograph landscapes, sunsets, portraits and night scenes.

Most photographers, when they have successfully mastered the art of taking good photographs, want also to take charge of processing their film. The final section of the book deals with developing and printing colour transparencies and negatives at home, to provide a complete encyclopedia of colour photography.

8 COLOUR AND LIGHT

Sunlight, or white light, is a mixture of all the colours in the visible spectrum. It is, in fact, a range of wavelengths of electromagnetic radiation, the shortest being violet and the longest red. These wavelengths are measured in nanometres – one millionth of a millimetre – and only the narrow band between about 400 and 700 nanometres can be seen by the human eye. Shorter than 400 is ultraviolet, which, although invisible to us, can affect colour film. Longer than 700 is infra-red, which again, although undetected by our eyesight, can be recorded by specially sensitized film.

The colours in the visible spectrum are red, orange, yellow, green, blue, indigo and violet. However, it can be conveniently divided into just three primary colours, red, green and blue. If three lights of equal intensity are fitted with a red, green and a blue filter and are projected onto the same spot the result will be white light. All the other colours can be produced by mixing the primaries in varying quantities.

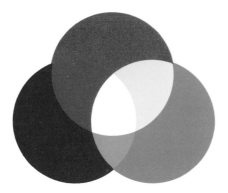

Above This schematic diagram shows how white light is formed from three primary colours adding to each other.
Right The familiar miracle of a rainbow clearly demonstrates the make-up of daylight. The droplets of water in the atmosphere act like a prism and split the white light up into its component colours.

Q How do we see coloured objects?
A When white light falls onto a coloured surface, a green leaf for instance, it reflects only the wavelengths in the green area of the spectrum. All the other wavelengths are absorbed and converted into heat.

Q Why do some things appear to be a different colour when viewed under different lights?
A Because some light sources, such as fluorescent tubes and mercury vapour lamps, do not emit all the wavelengths that are present in sunlight.

Q Why can sunlight sometimes vary in colour, such as at sunset?
A Because the Earth's atmosphere filters out or absorbs some of the wavelengths. The degree of absorption depends on weather conditions in the atmosphere and the direction of the sunlight. In the late afternoon, sunlight hits the atmosphere at a more acute angle than at midday and so has to pass through more of the atmosphere to reach us.

10 HOW COLOUR FILM WORKS

Colour film works on the same basic principle as black and white film: a light-sensitive emulsion creates an image according to the intensity of the light falling on it. The difference is that in a colour film there are three separate layers of emulsion, one sensitive to only red light, one to green and the other to blue. At a particular stage in the processing, these individual images are dyed to the appropriate shade and combine to reproduce the full range of colours present in the original subject.

There are two basic types of colour film, transparency (for slides) and negative (for prints). A negative film records light areas in the original subject as a dark tone and vice versa. It also shows the colours in reverse so that anything red will appear as a mixture of green and blue, which is called cyan, anything green will record as a mixture of red and blue, called magenta, and anything blue as a mixture of red and green, which is yellow. These are known as the complementary colours. To make a print, the colour negative must then be exposed again to a similar emulsion on a paper base to convert the tones and colours back to those of the original subject.

With a colour transparency film, all of this process takes place – including the reversal of tones and colours – when the film is developed.

Q Why can I not see these complementary colours clearly when I look at a colour negative?
A Because the film also contains a special masking layer to correct inherent faults in the dyes and this has an overall orange cast.

Q There appear to be many other different types of colour film than just negative and transparency. Why is this?
A There is no fundamental difference, it is a question of film speed. Both basic types can be obtained in a variety of speeds which makes them more suitable for different levels of light. Transparency film can be bought for use in either daylight or artificial light.

Q How does polaroid colour film work?
A The processing chemicals are incorporated into the film and are activated by pressure after exposure.

Above A schematic presentation of primary and secondary printing colours.
Left An accurate reproduction of the original colours of the subject.
Below left The subject printed in one primary colour – cyan.
Below right The same photograph printed in two primary colours – cyan and magenta.

12 HOW COLOUR FILM WORKS

Colour film is very sensitive to even slight changes in the colour quality of the light. Unfortunately, we tend only to notice when there is a drastic variation because the brain makes adjustments for what we see; a piece of white paper will almost always appear to be white, regardless of the colour of the light used to illuminate it, simply because we *know* it is white. We are very rarely aware of any changes in the colour quality of daylight, yet it varies considerably and colour film will faithfully record such variations. This accounts for many of the surprises – and disappointments – which you may experience when you see your pro-

cessed film for the first time.

The colour quality of light is measured in degrees Kelvin and is known as *colour temperature*. Most daylight-type colour films are designed to give a correct balance of colour when the light source is approximately 6000° Kelvin. However, the light from a rising or setting sun can be as low as 3000° and as high as 8000° from a hazy or overcast sky. When you consider that a variation of only 200° will be quite noticeable when recorded on colour film, it is easy to understand how sometimes a photograph can be quite a different colour from the scene you thought you saw.

Above *Marrakesh market after sundown. This scene shows how film can record the cool blue quality which is a result of a high colour temperature.*

Right *The warm glow of this Maltese harbour scene was created by the light of a late afternoon sun. Much of the blue wavelengths of light had been absorbed by the atmosphere.*

Q Can I use daylight film when taking flash pictures?
A Yes provided you are using either electronic flash or blue tinted flash bulbs, which are specially balanced to match daylight film.

Q Can I use colour correction filters with both colour negative and transparency film?
A As a general rule it is not necessary to use correction filters in daylight conditions when shooting negative film since the correction can be made at the printing stage.

Q Why do distant views often have a bluish quality?
A Because more ultraviolet light is usually present in such situations. Atmospheric haze compounds the effect. This is particularly noticeable at high altitudes.

14 CHOOSING COLOUR FILM

It is important to choose the most suitable type of colour film for your particular purpose in order to obtain the best possible results. Your first choice is between colour negative and colour transparency (positive) film. If colour prints are your main requirement, then colour negative film is the most obvious choice, since the cost of producing prints from negatives is lower than from transparency film, and the quality is higher (unless very expensive, professional prints are made from transparencies). If you are inexperienced, colour negative film can also be preferable since there is more latitude for exposure and minor errors to be corrected in the printing process. If you intend to process you own film and make your own colour prints, you will learn more about the process and how to control it by using the negative-positive process.

If your main requirement is for colour transparencies – either for projection or for selling your pictures for reproduction (colour prints are rarely used for this) – then you should use transparency film. Although it is possible to make slides from negatives there is an inevitable loss of quality.

When you have decided on the type of film, the next consideration is speed. Your choice depends mainly on the lighting conditions you intend to shoot in.

You should also remember that image quality and sharpness are much greater with a slower, fine-grained film than with the high-speed variety. The difference between Kodachrome 25 for instance and, say, an ISO 400/27 film is very noticeable indeed, so in normal circumstances do not use a faster film than the lighting conditions require.

Above This architectural detail was illuminated by bright sunlight and an exposure of 1/125 second at f8 was possible even with ISO 25/15 Kodachrome.

Right A fast film is often an unavoidable choice for subjects which combine a need for a fast shutter speed and a low light level such as this surfer.

Q Is there much difference between similar types and speeds of transparency film from different makers?
A There can indeed be and it is wise, if you are a beginner, to experiment with a few different makes to determine which gives the most pleasing rendition.

Q Is it always best to use a fast film in dull light?
A Not necessarily. If your subject is static and you are able to give longer exposures, with a landscape for instance, then it can be better to use a slower, fine-grained film since the extra image quality and often greater contrast can give a lift to softly lit scenes.

Q What is film speed?
A Film speed indicates the relative sensitivity of the film to a given light level. A film which has twice the speed will need half the exposure to produce the same result.

Q Why is film speed important?
A Because if you don't know the speed of the film you cannot determine the correct exposure. You must set the film speed number on the camera or exposure meter before it can give a relevant exposure indication.

Q What does ISO mean?
A The ISO rating combines two separate methods of measurement, DIN and ASA. ISO 100/21 is the same as 21 DIN or ASA 100.

Q What is DIN?
A This is the European system. Doubling of film speed is indicated by an increase of three, so that 21 DIN is twice the speed of 18 DIN, and so on.

Q What is ASA?
A This is the American system. Doubling of the film speed is indicated by doubling the number. So 100 ASA is twice the speed of 50 ASA and so on.

Q Can film be uprated in the camera?
A Yes, since the decision is not made until the film is processed. You cannot, of course, alter the speed of individual frames, so the speed must be set to the new rating before you start shooting.

Q What is 'pushing' in the processing stage?
A This involves using increased development time or special developers which increase the sensitivity or speed of the film beyond that which is marked on the packet.

Q Are some films more amenable to this treatment than others?
A Yes. Colour transparency more than colour negative and fast films more than slow.

16 FILTERS FOR COLOUR

There are essentially two main types of filter for use with colour film: correction filters, which are used to avoid a colour cast as a result of the lighting quality being different to that for which the film is balanced; and effects filters, which are used to deliberately create a colour cast.

The most useful colour correction filters are the UV (ultraviolet) and the skylight, which counteract the blue cast caused on cloudy days and in open shade. For a stronger effect, choose the 81A or 81B. The 82A and 82B filters are also useful for reducing the warm colour cast created when shooting in the even-

ing light. It is also possible to buy filters which enable daylight film to be used in artificial lighting and vice versa.

The polarizing filter is particularly useful in colour photography since it reduces the light which is reflected from surfaces such as water and foliage. It also helps to create stronger and brighter colours and will make a blue sky a deeper colour. Graduated filters are very effective in creating dramatic skies such as sunsets and can be bought in a range of colours as well as grey. Only half of the filter is tinted so that it can be used to alter the sky but not the foreground.

Above A Wratten 81B filter was used for this shot of a girl taken in open shade on a sunny day.
Right above Two graduated filters were used for this into-the-light shot, a neutral to reduce the brightness of the sky and a tobacco to add a little colour.

Right A polarizing filter was used to increase the density and colour saturation of the blue sky in this Hawaiian seascape.

Q Do you need to give extra exposure when using filters for colour?
A The pale filters such as the UV and the skylight require no increase, but the more dense filters such as the polarizing need additional exposure according to the filter factor.

Q Can you use black and white filters for colour photography?
A Only for special effects, since they will create a strong colour cast.

Q Can you use a polarizing filter for black and white pictures?
A Yes. It will reduce unwanted reflections and glare.

Q Will TTL metering adjust the exposure for colour filters?
A Yes.

18 FILTERS FOR COLOUR

One of the most effective ways of modifying and controlling the colour quality of an image is to use colour filters. These are simply glass or plastic squares or discs, tinted in a range of colours, which can be mounted onto the front of the lens. A modest selection of these filters is basic equipment for the photographer who wishes to produce more than just a record of a scene. There are now a number of systems available which allow you to collect a more than adequate selection of filters and effects attachments at a reasonable cost. With the aid of different mounts, these can be used on a number of different lenses and cameras.

The first basic is the *UV filter*, the one which many photographers leave in position on their lenses all the time; although it is intended to reduce the effects of ultraviolet light, it will not have a detrimental effect when there is none present and it does afford protection to the far more costly lens. The second filter which

should be in every photographer's kit is the *81A colour correction filter*. This is a pale, straw colour and offsets the blue cast created when shooting on overcast days and in open shade. It also reduces the effect of ultraviolet light, and some photographers use it in place of a UV filter. You might also find it useful to pack the stronger versions of this filter, the *81B* and the *81C*, for more extreme conditions.

Although less frequently needed, the *82A or B filter* can also be useful when the light source would otherwise create a warm cast, such as early evening sunlight, or when shooting in normal room lighting on tungsten type film. In addition, it can be handy to have the *conversion filters* from tungsten to daylight and vice versa for those occasions when you find you have the wrong type of film loaded into your camera. These are the *80A* for daylight film in tungsten light and the *85B* for tungsten type film in daylight.

Above *A polarizing filter was used to enhance the effect of the dramatic sky. As well as making the sky a richer and deeper blue, it has also emphasized the clouds.*

Right *These two pictures show the effect of a tobacco-coloured graduated filter used to add colour to the blank sky tone of a lake scene. The exposure was calculated before fitting the filter.*

20 DAYLIGHT AND COLOUR

When you are working with a light source of a substantially higher colour temperature than that for which the film is manufactured, the resulting photographs will have a bluish colour cast. This is commonly seen on pictures taken on cloudy, overcast days. When the light source is of a lower colour temperature the result is a reddish cast, which is seen frequently on pictures taken in evening light. The former is known by photographers as a cool cast and the latter as warm. You can buy a special meter, similar to an exposure meter but designed to measure colour temperature, but for most purposes this is not necessary. It is perfectly possible – and fun – simply to teach yourself to become aware of these colour casts and anticipate the problems. As a general rule, a slight warm cast is quite acceptable, but a bluish or cold cast can be rather unpleasant and is best avoided. In most circumstances colour correction filters will compensate for the colour cast – a bluish filter to balance a warm cast and a reddish filter to offset a cool cast. Sometimes a colour cast can contribute to the atmosphere and effect of a picture, and you should always consider this before you attempt to .counteract it.

In addition to the variations caused by the colour temperature of the daylight itself it is also important to be aware of two other potential hazards. One is the presence of the invisible ultraviolet radiations which can create a blue cast on colour film. The other is the possibility of a colour cast produced by light being reflected from brightly coloured surfaces near the subject. A common instance of this is the bluish light reflected from the sky when taking pictures in open shade.

Right Ultraviolet lights in this mountain scene has resulted in the picture having a marked bluish cast, more so than would have been apparent to the eye.

22 DAYLIGHT AND COLOUR

Probably the most difficult conditions under which to take successful colour photographs are the very ones that most inexperienced photographers favour — a bright sunny day. While such lighting can produce good pictures, it needs more than a little care to avoid the pitfalls.

Bright sunlight unfortunately tends to create a much higher contrast than the film can accommodate, with strong highlights and dense shadows. Pictures taken in the close to middle distance in particular will tend to have a harsh and unpleasing quality unless care is taken to control the angle and direction of the lighting. Our eyes are able to adjust to extremes of contrast and it is easy to forget that the film's latitude is being exceeded. A useful trick to help judge this factor is to view the subject through half-closed eyes. Sometimes the difficulty is easily overcome. When photographing a friend, for instance, it is a simple matter to ask them to move to a different position where the lighting is less harsh. In other cases more favourable lighting must be achieved by the choice of camera viewpoint.

It is important to avoid situations where the distribution of highlight and shadow in the subject is equal, since such pictures will inevitably contain large areas where highlights are burnt out and shadows are dense and lacking in detail. Choose a viewpoint where the subject is either predominantly in shadow or the shadows are very small, and calculate the exposure accordingly.

Right This shot of schoolchildren was taken from a position where the major part of the subject was in shadow and the exposure calculated accordingly. The small area of resulting overexposure is insignificant.
Far right The position of this man's head and the camera viewpoint were selected so that, although lit by direct sunlight, the shadows cast were minimal and did not create an unpleasant effect. This type of lighting is often more effective for a weathered, tanned skin than for a pale, smooth one.

Q What use is the lenshood in these circumstances?

A A lenshood prevents bright light striking the lens and causing flare. Anything which casts a shadow over the camera lens – your hand for example – will have a similar, sometimes better effect than a lenshood, providing it does not encroach on the picture area.

Q Must the sun always be behind the photographer?

A By no means. The position of the sun relative to the camera and the subject should be considered in terms of its overall effect and the nature of the shadows it casts.

Q Can heat affect film?

A Yes. Apart from light, heat is the most damaging thing to film. Don't leave your camera in the sun.

24 ARTIFICIAL LIGHT AND COLOUR

Artificial light can be provided by a number of sources suitable for colour photography, but, like daylight, there are some variations in the relative colour temperatures. Most films designed for use in tungsten light are balanced to give optimum results with a colour temperature of 3200° Kelvin, the temperature produced by a floodlight bulb or a tungsten halogen lamp. An overrun bulb such as a photoflood produces a slightly higher colour temperature and a normal domestic bulb a slightly lower one. If you wish to use photoflood bulbs for your colour slide photography, buy the tungsten type A film, which is designed for the slightly bluer quality. The type B film is balanced for the warmer studio bulbs and can also be used in normal room lighting.

It is possible to use daylight type film when shooting with tungsten lighting, provided you use the appropriate compensation filter. However, this will require an increase in exposure and it is preferable to use the correct film for the light source whenever possible.

Other types of artificial lighting should be avoided where critical results are required, such as portraits. Fluorescent tubes, whether the so-called daylight type or the warm light, will produce a heavy colour cast when used with either daylight or tungsten type film because they do not emit all the wavelengths of the visible spectrum and require quite heavy filtration to produce an acceptable result.

Above left Urban glitter illuminated solely by artificial light and taken on artificial light film, resulting in a fairly accurate rendition.
Above right This detail of an office block photographed in daylight on daylight type film shows clearly how the white fluorescent lights inside the offices have recorded – distinctly green.
Right The Casino at Baden-Baden was photographed on daylight type film. The predominant tungsten light has created a pronounced orange cast.

Q What type of film should I use for street scenes at night?
A It will depend to a great extent on the nature of the predominant street lighting. Sodium or mercury vapour lamps, for example, are virtually monochromatic. Sodium lamps produce primarily the yellow wavelengths, making tungsten film a best choice. Mercury produces mainly the blue-green range and daylight film will give a more pleasing result.

Q What should I use if I do not know what the light source is?
A If in doubt use daylight film, since a warm cast will create a more natural effect than a blue cast.

Q What is an overrun bulb?
A It is a bulb which is designed to produce a higher intensity of light for its wattage in exchange for a shorter life – a few hours instead of several hundred for a conventional bulb.

Q Should I use artificial light film when photographing something like a rock concert?
A It is almost impossible to judge the quality of the constantly variable lighting used for stage effects and consequently the film type used is usually not at all important. Many photographers prefer to use daylight type film in these circumstances.

26 LIGHT AND THE TIME OF DAY

The nature and the quality of daylight can vary considerably. One of the most important variables is the effect of the time of day. At noon the sun is at its highest point in the sky and if there are no clouds the shadows it casts are very small and intense. In the early morning and evening, when the sun is close to the horizon it produces much longer and larger shadows. In landscape photography, for instance, the light of a midday sun can often create a rather flat effect, with little impression of form and texture. The same scene photographed in, say, evening light is frequently transformed, with the contours of the landscape thrown into sharp relief and the impression of texture greatly enhanced. Even a portrait can be affected by this change in the lighting. Often noon sunlight creates a very harsh and excessive top light with dense shadows under the eyes and chin, whereas when the light comes from a lower angle a more pleasing and flattering effect is created.

Do remember that the *colour* of the light changes during the day as well as the quality, and early and late in the day it will be more red than at noon.

Left The low angle of the sunlight in this evening shot has emphasized the shapes and texture of the image as well as creating a warm, atmospheric quality. **Below** The textural quality of the hillside in this landscape shot has been created by the late afternoon sunlight, which literally skates across its surface picking out almost every blade of grass. **Right** Noon sunlight has created a quite stark quality emphasizing the harsh, hot quality of this Moroccan landscape.

Q How can you correct the reddish cast created by evening sunlight?
A By using a colour correction filter in the Wratten 82 range. The 82A is the weakest, and the 82B and 82C progressively stronger.

Q Should you always use a colour correction filter when shooting early or late in the day?
A By no means. The warm cast created by this light is often contributory to the atmosphere of such pictures.

Q What pictures need to be corrected?
A Portraits can look unpleasant with a strong colour cast because skin tones in particular make the effect more noticeable.

28 MIXED LIGHTING

Although film manufacturers conveniently divide film types into daylight and artificial, in real life things are not so neatly arranged. Two or more different sources are often used in the same picture. The decision as to which type of film to use under these conditions should normally be based on the predominant light source. For example, if you are taking a portrait using tungsten light to illuminate your model, but there is a small amount of daylight visible through a window in the background, then your choice should be tungsten type film since this will create natural looking skin tones and the small area of bluish daylight would be quite acceptable. However, if the scene was lit predominantly by daylight and only a small area of it was illuminated by tungsten light, then daylight film should be used.

In some circumstances, it is possible to use colour filters or acetates over one of the light sources to balance them. You could, for instance, fit a yellowish daylight to tungsten conversion filter over an electronic flash gun so that it could be mixed with tungsten lighting. You can also buy sheets of blue-tinted acetate which can be placed over artificial light sources so that they can be mixed with daylight. Do not, however, overlook the atmospheric effects of mixed lighting. Sometimes the 'wrong' choice of film can enhance this: for example, an illuminated building photographed at dusk would, for a correct result, require the use of tungsten type film, but the warm glow created by using daylight type film may well produce a more atmospheric picture.

Right The rich colours of this Las Vegas sign were enhanced by shooting at dusk and by using daylight type film. This has helped to create the blue cast of the background as well as adding to the effect of the tungsten light.
Far right The glow of candlelight has created a distinctly warm cast on this woman's face, although the room itself was lit by tungsten lighting and tungsten type film was used. It could have been corrected by the use of a filter, but unfiltered it contributes to the mood of the picture.

Q What film should I use if daylight and artificial light are evenly mixed?
A In most circumstances, daylight type film is the safest choice simply because as a general rule a blue cast is less pleasing than a yellow cast.

Q Why is it not possible to buy colour negative film for use in tungsten light?
A Because for most normal purposes it is possible to correct the colour balance at the printing stage. You can, however, buy a type L colour negative film for use with the longer exposures often needed when shooting in artificial light.

Q Is it best to use colour negative or slide film when shooting with mixed lighting?
A Colour negative film will give you the opportunity to decide on the final balance of colour at the printing stage, whereas once you have exposed slide film it is not possible to alter it substantially.

Q Are some slide films better than others for mixed lighting scenes?
A As a general rule, the faster films such as the Kodak ISO 400/27 are more tolerant of variations in colour balance than slower films such as Kodachrome.

30 EXPOSURE AND COLOUR

Deciding on the right exposure is one of the most important considerations in producing consistently good quality pictures. Most modern exposure meters if used sensibly will produce an acceptable result under most conditions. With a subject of normal contrast, that is to say within the latitude of the film, a correct exposure is one that records adequate detail in both the darker and lighter tones of the image. However, in many situations the subject contrast is often higher or lower than the norm and in these cases 'correct' exposure becomes a more subjective decision. Even when a scene has an average contrast range, the exposure that will create the most pleasing effect is not necessarily the correct one.

If less exposure is given than that indicated by the exposure meter, the immediate effect is to produce a denser transparency than normal or a thinner negative. In addition, there will often be an increase in image contrast and the colours will be more saturated. With a softly lit subject the effect will be to create a more low key, sombre image and with a contrasty subject the result will be a more dramatic quality, with dense shadows but full detail in the high-

lights. A degree of underexposure often suits subjects where there is a bold element of texture in the lighter tones of the subject, such as the weathered skin in a portrait of an old man. It can also give emphasis to pictures where the shape of the subject is an important element by creating a slightly silhouetted effect. Where there is a dramatic sky or a colourful sunset, less exposure than normal will create richer tones and stronger colours.

Giving more exposure than the meter indicates will have the opposite effect. It will produce a lighter transparency than normal and a colour negative will be more dense. There will be a loss of detail in the lighter tones of the subject and a gain in shadow detail; colours will be softer and more pastel; there will usually be a lowering of image contrast, and the overall effect will be to create a picture with a more delicate and gentle mood than that of a normal or underexposed image. A degree of overexposure is often an advantage in portraits where you wish to minimize the effect of skin texture, such as a glamour shot for instance, or where romantic mood will enhance the picture, such as a misty landscape.

Above A bracketed exposure in which additional exposures are made each side of that calculated to be correct. In this case half a stop under and half a stop over.

Right This close-up of peppers on a market stall was underexposed by about half a stop to ensure that the colour was fully saturated.

Q Is there any other way of varying the exposure without bracketing?

A If you use colour negative film, it is possible to make the print slightly lighter or darker without loss of quality. With colour transparencies, it is possible to shoot a whole roll of film on a similar subject, such as a portrait for instance, and to cut off one frame from the end and process it as a test. The remainder of the film can then be adjusted during the processing. Most transparency films can be made at least half a stop darker and up to two stops or more lighter.

Q What is the best way of taking an exposure reading?

A For a subject of normal contrast most TTL meters will give an accurate reading. So will any other type of separate meter, such as a handheld one, provided you make sure that it 'sees' only the area you are photographing and any large light or dark areas such as sky are excluded.

Q How do you take a reading for a high contrast subject?

A You can either take a close-up reading from a mid tone in the subject, or you can take an average of readings from the lightest and darkest areas.

Q How can I bracket exposures with my automatic camera?

A By simply altering the film speed setting: if you are using an ISO 100/21 and you set your film speed dial to ISO 50/18, you will be overexposing by one stop; if you set it to ISO 200/24 you will be underexposing by one stop, and so on.

Q Can disasters be rescued at the processing stage?

A If you know that you have over- or underexposed a roll of film, by setting it to the wrong ISO for instance, it can be pushed or held back in processing to a degree.

32 EXPOSURE AND COLOUR

The most effective way to learn how to control the quality of your pictures by the use of exposure is to *bracket* your exposures wherever possible. This involves making three or four exposures of a subject at half stop intervals each side of the setting indicated by the exposure meter. In this way you will be able to see just how much a particular subject can be improved by giving more or less exposure than normal. At the same time you can familiarize yourself with the characteristics of the film you use and be able to predict your results more accurately.

Above *Extreme overexposure has been used in this portrait to achieve the bleached effect, the skin recording with no detail. In this case one and a half stops extra exposure was given.*
Right *The dramatic effect of these backlit rocks has been created by underexposing by one stop. The shadows have recorded as a rich black, the texture is emphasized and the highlights accentuated.*

34 COLOUR AND MOOD

Colour can have a very considerable effect on our feelings and moods. Modern marketing techniques make full use of the psychological effects of colour, from the decor of shops to the design of packaging. An understanding of the relationship between colour and mood is just as important to the photographer, who is concerned with producing expressive and atmospheric pictures.

The spectrum in fact expresses a range of moods as well as colours. Red, for instance, is a colour which we connect with warning and danger and as such it is the most dominant colour in the spectrum. Orange and yellow have a much less threatening aspect and their warm qualities tend to create an inviting or cosy atmosphere, like the amber glow of a log fire, for example. The cooler colours of green and blue are the predominant colours of nature and evoke a restful and reassuring response. Indigo and violet on the other hand have a much more sombre and subdued quality.

In addition to the colours themselves their degree of saturation and the way they are combined will also affect the mood they create. Full-blooded colours have a bright and lively quality, whereas soft pastel colours have a more gentle and romantic nature. Darker toned colours, like brown for instance, induce a rather serious or sad mood. For these reasons it is important that the colour quality of your pictures enhances the mood you wish to create. A picture of a lively group of children playing, for example, would be enhanced if they were wearing brightly coloured clothes and diminished if they wore drab and dull colours.

Q How can you control the colour and the mood of a picture?
A The main way is by choosing viewpoints and by framing the picture so that the most effective colours are emphasized and ones which spoil the mood are excluded. With some pictures, such as portraits or still lifes, you can actually select colours so that they contribute to a particular mood.

Q Can you use filters to control colour and mood?
A In some circumstances you can use colour correction filters to create a colour cast, such as a warm evening light, so that it adds to the atmosphere of a shot. Soft focus attachments and fog filters can be used to make colours paler and softer to create a more romantic mood.

Q Are there any exercises to train my eye?
A Look at advertisements, films and paintings and observe how they use colour to establish mood.

Left The peaceful mood of this landscape is emphasized by the subtle colour quality of the shades of green. The gentle contours have also contributed to the atmosphere.

Below The rather low-key quality of this picture combined with the subdued colour range of purple and brown adds emphasis to the flower lady's expression and the sombre mood of the picture.

36 DOMINANT COLOUR

In many photographs the colour content of the image is largely a secondary element. The subject itself is the main point of the picture and the colour is an element of the composition. Yet colour itself can be an effective subject for a picture, other elements such as shape, form or texture and the subject itself being subordinated to a relatively minor role.

Such pictures can be created in a variety of ways. The most basic is to move in very close to your subject or to frame it tightly with a long focus lens so that the picture is literally filled with colour, like a close-up of a pile of fruit on a market stall for instance. Another way is to use a very small but bold area of colour set against a large area of contrasting colour or neutral toned background, like a tiny, red-sailed boat on a wide expanse of blue sea.

The essential point is that there should be a dominant colour in such images so that when someone looks at the picture they will immediately see that colour above all else. To look for pictures of this type is an excellent way of teaching yourself to become colour conscious and to learn how to isolate and control the element of colour in your photographs. You can experiment for example with making the area of colour in the image as small as possible while still remaining the dominant element or seeing how much of one colour you can use before the picture becomes meaningless or boring.

Above Although the element of colour in this picture is tiny, it has a powerful effect. It has been placed in a strong part of the image and it is contrasted against an unobtrusive background.

Right Yellow is the immediate impression of this shot. A careful choice of viewpoint and framing has allowed the bright yellow umbrellas to dominate the composition with colour.

Q Are there any techniques that will help to make colours more dominant?
A A small degree of underexposure will often help to make colours record as a richer hue. You should avoid lighting that creates strong highlights.

Q Can filters be used to make colour more dominant?
A In some situations it is possible to use a colour correction filter of the same hue as the dominant colour to give it more emphasis. A polarising filter can also emphasize colour.

Q Are some colours naturally more dominant?
A Yes. The warm colours, red in particular but also orange and yellow, tend to be more dominant. A fully saturated colour is more dominant than a weak colour.

38 MIXED COLOURS

Perhaps the most difficult subject to photograph satisfactorily is one that contains a mixture of bright colours. Yet it is unfortunately the one to which the inexperienced in particular are most attracted. When a variety of bright colours are massed together they tend to clash with each other, creating discord, and to fight for attention, producing a confusing and unbalanced image. This does not mean that you should not attempt to tackle such subjects or limit your photography to subjects with only two or three different colours, but rather that you should learn to be more disciplined and selective in your approach to this type of picture.

One way of controlling a mass of bold colours in a picture is to frame it with an area of a fairly neutral tone or colour. A mixed flower border, for instance, would look more pleasing if you moved back with your camera to allow, say, the dark green of the lawn to surround it rather than more mixed colours of other flowers. A multicoloured subject will often work well when it can be set against a very light or dark surrounding area.

In some instances it is possible to impose a feeling of order on a random riot of colours simply by the careful choice of a viewpoint and selective framing. Differential focussing is an effective way to reduce a fussily multicoloured background to a more neutral tone by throwing it out of focus.

Above The white background provided by the snow in this colourful picture of skiers has helped to contain and organize the bold mixed colours of the subject.

Right Tight framing and the element of pattern has created a sense of order from this display of Mexican paper flowers. Without care, such a subject could easily become a jumble of colour.

40 RESTRICTING COLOUR RANGE

The temptation in colour photography is to always respond to the subjects which contain boldly defined colours. However, there is considerable scope in subjects that have a very restricted colour range, either because of a combination of muted colours or because they are essentially monochromatic. Pictures of this type are invariably able to convey mood and atmosphere more successfully. Subjects which are dependent on dominant elements such as shape, pattern, texture and form are likely to have more impact when this is not confused by an excess of colour. Some of the most successful pictures of this type are in fact almost black and white with only a suggestion of colour.

This type of photograph can be achieved in two basic ways. The first is when the subject itself is restricted in colour, such as a landscape in shades of green, for instance, or a carefully arranged still life in which all the ingredients have been selected because of their common colour values. The other way is to light a subject which itself contains a variety of colours in such a way that they appear muted. Weather or atmospheric conditions reduce the strength and saturation of the colours to create an impression of one colour. Mist, fog and rain can often achieve this and shooting into the light can produce the same effect.

Above *Careful framing has ensured that there are no bold contrasts in this picture. The lack of obtrusive colour has helped to emphasize the pattern.*
Right *Although this shot is almost monochromatic the slight hint of colour gives it a subtle, textural quality.*

42 SHOOTING IN LOW LIGHT

Many photographers simply put their cameras away when the light level drops below a point at which they can safely handhold their cameras, and the slower shutter speeds of their cameras are never used. This is a great pity, since many interesting and atmospheric lighting effects are created when the sun has gone down or the light is poor.

A firm tripod is an invaluable accessory. It can greatly increase your picture-making opportunities by enabling you to give longer exposures and make use of low light levels. City streets at night, illuminated buildings, dusk and moonlight pictures are well within the scope of even a simple camera on a tripod.

There are two main pitfalls to be avoided on this type of shot. The first is the very high contrast that night shots in particular tend to have. Care is needed to avoid pictures with large areas of black void and burnt-out highlights. With subjects like illuminated streets and buildings, for instance, it is best to take pictures before it is completely dark so that some ambient light remains to illuminate the sky and retain some detail in the shadows. The other factor to be aware of is exposure. Extreme contrast can mislead the meter, so a good method is to take an average of readings from the darkest and lightest areas and to avoid actual light sources like street lamps. You must also allow for *reciprocity failure* when giving exposures longer than about half a second or so.

Above *An exposure of one second was needed for this shot of a circus tent at night, using ISO 400/27 film with the camera mounted on a tripod. The exposure was calculated by the averaging method.*

Above right *This picture, taken well after the sun had gone down, required twice the exposure indicated because of reciprocity failure.*
Right *The moon rising over Yosemite. The exposure was calculated by taking a reading from the sky above the camera.*

Q What is reciprocity failure?
A It happens when the film becomes less sensitive in proportion to the increase of exposure time. Most films begin to show signs of this with exposures in excess of about half a second. For example, a film may be rated at ISO 100/21 but at one second exposures it may drop to ISO 64/19 and at five seconds to ISO 32/16 and so on. The effect varies from film to film. It is sensible to do some tests with your usual stock at various exposure times as the colour balance can also shift and you may need to compensate with colour correction filters.

44 USING A SOFTER LIGHT

Even on a sunny day, the quality of the lighting can vary quite considerably. The light of a bright unobscured sun in a deep blue sky for example will create a much more contrasty lighting than when there are a number of large white clouds around or when there is a slight haze. When the sun is lower in the sky the shadows may be larger but they are also less dense and the light is usually softer and mellower. The ˚surroundings, too, will affect the quality of the light. Where your subject is in an essentially light-toned setting – on a beach for example – there will be a considerable amount of the sunlight scattered and reflected into the shadow areas, reducing the brightness range.

Open shade is also an effective way of finding a softer light on a sunny day, since the subject will be shielded from the direct light of the sun and will be lit only by reflected light. When taking a portrait, for instance, you can position your model in the shade of a building or a tree. A problem in this situation is however that since the subject is being lit predominantly by light reflected from a blue sky, there will inevitably be a blue cast on the film unless a colour correction filter such as an 81A or B is used.

The softest light is created when the sky is overcast or when there is mist. Inexperienced photographers often put their cameras away on such days, yet these conditions can produce an ideal illumination for very colourful subjects, especially where a more subtle mood is required.

Above *The mood of this Italian lake scene was largely created by shooting in the soft light of dusk. It appeared quite different earlier in the day in bright sunlight.*

Right *Even in the harsh light of the sun, it is still possible to find a softer light by shooting subjects in open shade as in this shot of a market. An 81A filter was used.*

46 USING MIXED LIGHTING

When you are shooting black and white pictures there is no problem about mixing light from different sources, but with colour film this can cause a noticeable effect. For instance, if you are taking a picture indoors using daylight, but you also use some tungsten lighting to boost the daylight, one or other of these sources will create a colour cast. If you shoot on daylight film, the area illuminated by daylight will record naturally, but the part of the subject lit by the tungsten light will have an orange cast. If you shoot on artificial light film, the area lit by the tungsten light will appear normal, but the details illuminated by the daylight will have a blue cast. The answer is to choose the film type to match the colour quality of the predominant light source and to make sure that they are not evenly balanced. As a rule, the effect is more acceptable when there is a warm cast than it is when there is a blue cast, so daylight type film is the safest choice.

If you are using a small source of mixed light, such as a flash gun, with tungsten light you can fit a colour conversion filter over the flash gun so that it matches the colour quality of the artificial light.

Above Tungsten light film was used for this picture. Although the illuminated room appears almost correct in colour, the residual daylight has produced a blue cast.
Above right This interior was lit with an almost equal mixture of tungsten light and daylight. It was photographed on daylight type film, resulting in a warm cast where the artificial light is strongest.
Right Tungsten light film was also used for this street scene. The sodium vapour lighting has created an orange cast, although the unlit areas are blue.

Q Can you mix fluorescent light with daylight?
A No. Although they appear similar, and some tubes are called daylight type, they are quite different to daylight and will produce a strong colour cast, usually green, unless filtered.

Q What sort of filter should I use for fluorescent light?
A There is considerable variation in the different types of tube. However, most fluorescent tubes are lacking in red, and with daylight type tubes using daylight type film a 30 to 40 magenta filter will usually produce an acceptable result. Where possible a test exposure is advisable.

48 USING DAYLIGHT INDOORS

Daylight can be an ideal source of light for indoor photography. The essential thing is, of course, a good-sized window or skylight. If this is exposed to the direct light of the sun, you will need some means of diffusing it, a large sheet of tracing paper, for example, taped across the glass or even just a white net curtain.

Since the only way of controlling the direction of the light is to move your subject and the camera in relation to the window, you will also need to have a moveable background for subjects like portraits and a table or bench for still life pictures. When you set up your camera with the window behind it the result will be a frontal light with few shadows and little modelling. With the subject and camera arranged so that the window is to one side, the effect will be a more directional light with greater modelling and quite pronounced shadows. Since this will tend to create excessive contrast, you will also need a large white reflector which can be placed close to the subject on the shadow side and angled to reflect the window light back into the shadows. This can be a piece of white card or polystyrene simply propped against a chair. Mirrors can also be used to create a stronger effect.

A tripod will be particularly useful for indoor work. It will help to avoid camera shake at the inevitable slow speeds you will need. You can also use it to support the camera, set up and ready to shoot, leaving you free to study lighting effects at your leisure and make any necessary adjustments.

Above Taken inside the clown's caravan this portrait was lit by windows on each side and at the rear to provide a white background.
Above right For a more dramatic effect, the model in this portrait was positioned almost at right angles to the window, creating a quite strongly-lit profile with dense shadows.

Right Soft but directional daylight from a window provides a light which has effectively emphasized the textural quality of this simple still life.

Q What is the best background to use.
A You can buy from professional photographic dealers large rolls of cartridge paper in a range of colours. These can be supported by threading a piece of wooden dowelling through the core and resting each end on two light stands or similar supports.

Q Can fabric be used as a background?
A Yes, but it must be crease free, otherwise it can look very unattractive and distracting.

Q Is indoor daylight suitable for colour photography?
A Yes, certainly, although you may find that you will need to use a faster film because of the lower light level and with a north facing window, or one that is illuminated by the sky, you will probably need to use a filter such as an 81A to offset a possible blue cast.

Today the vast majority of pictures taken by amateur photographers are in colour. In one sense, colour photography is easier than black and white. The film is exposed, then usually sent to a processing laboratory and the results appear with little further effort. In many ways it is too easy. The depressing result is that for all the colour film that is consumed, only a minute proportion of really good colour photographs is produced. The rest are just a jumbled confusion of colour, at best a poor record of an event or a scene. This is because colour is a very powerful element in an image and unless care and thought is given to the way it is organized and selected in a picture, the result will invariably be disappointing.

It is also an unfortunate fact that the very scenes that attract the inexperienced photographer are invariably those which are most unlikely to produce a satisfying photograph. Favourite disasters are vividly colourful scenes in bright sunshine with every colour in the rainbow indiscriminately scattered throughout them. Such situations require a very perceptive eye and a highly selective composition to produce an appealing image. A subject which contains only one or two boldly defined areas of colour against a neutral or contrasting background is far more likely to produce a prizewinning picture.

Above The impact of this picture depends on a highly selective approach. The only strong colour is red, the background is almost white and the image is framed tightly around the centre of interest.

Right Although more is included in this shot, it has been framed in such a way that neither the colour nor the elements of the subject compete for attention, but work together.

52 ISOLATING THE SUBJECT

The first step in taking a photograph – having seen something which appeals to you – is to identify the main point of interest. Many unsuccessful pictures are the result of the photographer simply not having made this basic decision. It may be something quite obvious like a person's face in a portrait, or an element a little more difficult to identify, such as a particular tree in a landscape picture perhaps.

In a good picture, the eye will be led to this main subject. In order to achieve this you must make sure that it is sufficiently isolated from the surrounding details of the image. The simplest way to do this is to move close to your subject so that irrelevant details are excluded or relegated to the background. Not being close enough to the subject is one of the commonest causes of disappointing pictures, particularly of subjects such as people and animals.

The second step is to make sure that your main subject stands out quite clearly from the background. This can be done in several ways. One is to arrange that there is a bold tonal or colour contrast between them. Pose a dark subject against a light background or shoot a bright subject on a dark background – a flower set against a foil of green leaves for example. Another effective method is to use differential focussing, which requires the subject itself to be in sharp focus but the background to be out of focus.

Lighting can also help to isolate the subject. A bold highlight around its edge for instance can often be achieved by shooting into the light.

Right *Tight framing has ensured that the attention is fully focussed on the tuba player in this picture, although other identifiable elements are visible.*
Far right above *Differential or selective focussing has enabled this old lady's face to be recorded in sharp relief and clearly isolated from a potentially fussy background.*
Far right below *A plain contrasting background has been used in this shot to ensure that the subject is in bold relief and clearly defined, and that there are no distracting elements to confuse the image.*

Q What is depth of field?
A It is the distance in front of and beyond the point at which you have focussed a lens which still appears acceptably sharp.

Q How can I be sure that my background is out of focus?
A First ensure that there is as much distance as possible between the subject and the background and then use a wide aperture to limit the depth of field. If possible use a long focus lens to emphasize this effect further.

54 COLOUR CLOSE-UPS

Colour photography lends itself particularly well to the close-up techniques. This is largely because there is an abundance of potential subject matter all around us that appears unremarkable until we take a closer look at it. Simple everyday objects such as fruit, flowers, ornaments and utensils and even small creatures can reveal an infinite variety of textures, patterns and colours when photographed in close-up.

Most cameras, apart from the very basic, will focus down to about half a metre. This can be adequate for some subjects, but you will give yourself much more scope with a close-up lens, which reduces the close focussing distance of the camera lens even further. For SLR owners a set of extension tubes, a bellows unit or a macro lens offers even more potential, enabling lifesize or even magnified images to be obtained.

A tripod is another vital accessory for close-up work, because the depth of field reduces drastically when the lens is focussed at close distances and you will need to use a small aperture and longer shutter speeds. With the tripod you can also set up, frame and focus your camera accurately and make small adjustments easily. You will often find it easier when shooting close-ups to focus by moving the camera closer to or further away from the subject rather than altering the lens focussing ring.

Do not forget when you are using extension tubes or a bellows unit to give more exposure to allow for the extension.

Right An extension tube was used for this close-up of a flower. Soft lighting has enhanced its colour, and a medium aperture was used to ensure that the flower itself was sharp while the background remained out of focus.

Far right A supplementary lens was used to move in close and emphasize the texture of this piece of dockside machinery, creating an almost abstract image. A small aperture was used to ensure adequate depth of field.

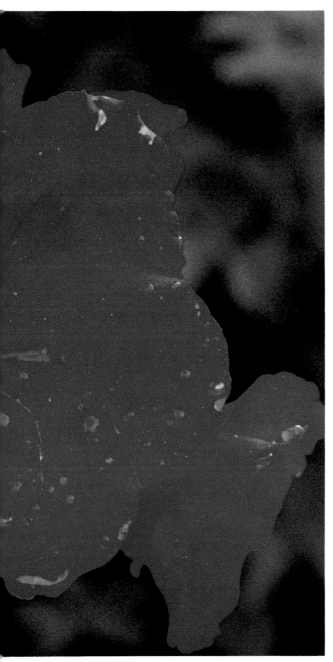

Q How do I calculate the exposure increase needed when using extension tubes?
A You must increase the exposure in proportion to the square of the increase in the distance the lens is extended beyond its focal length. For example, if a 50mm lens is extended so that it is 100mm from the film plane (ie twice the distance) then you must increase the exposure by four times. The formula is:

$$\left|\frac{\text{Total lens extension}}{\text{focal length of lens}}\right|^2 = \begin{array}{l}\text{increased}\\\text{exposure}\\\text{time}\end{array}$$

So taking the above example we have:

$$\left|\frac{100}{50}\right|^2 \doteqdot 2^2 = 4$$

Q Will I need a small aperture for close-up work?
A As a rule, yes, since the depth of field is much less with close-ups.

Q Will I need a cable release?
A A good idea. This is very useful when using slow shutter speeds as it prevents the camera being jarred when the shutter is released.

The type of view to which most people respond readily, the postcard vista of a summer landscape on a sunny day, is the one that is most difficult to translate successfully into an effective photograph. Our eyes are able to sweep over such a scene like a panning movie camera, building up an impression of it rather than making a factual record. But a factual record is exactly what the camera will record: usually there is no effective centre of interest and the result is an unsatisfactory image with no sense of order and composition.

It is essential to find or create a point in a landscape picture to which the eye will be led, such as a tree or a building. This can often be done by isolating a small area of a scene rather than attempting to include it all, and to frame it so that the other elements of the picture create a balance around the main point of interest. Where a broad view is essential a cohesive quality can often be created by introducing some foreground interest. This will help to create an impression of depth as well as leading the eye into the picture.

Lighting is a vital factor in landscape photography. Often an otherwise unremarkable scene can be transformed into a powerful image by a sudden change in the light. Shooting early or late in the day will help to create such situations when the low, slanting angle of the sun will reveal rich textures and patterns in the countryside. The light that occurs just after a storm can also be ideal for landscape photography.

Below left The elegant shapes of these bare trees create an impression of pattern which helps to make an effective composition. A long focus lens was used to isolate a small area of the scene.
Below A distant view is one of the most difficult subjects for a landscape picture. This shot was taken with a long focus lens to concentrate on a specific area of a wider view.

Q Do seascapes need a different technique?
A Not really. However, bear in mind the possibility of misleading exposure readings due to large areas of reflected light and highlights, and a possible blue cast resulting from ultraviolet light.

Q What is the best way of creating a feeling of distance in landscape shots?
A This can be done by including close foreground details in the frame to enhance the impression of perspective. This effect can be increased by using a wide angle lens.

Q Where is the best place to position the horizon in a landscape shot?
A As a general rule it is best to avoid a centrally placed horizon as this can create a picture which is too evenly balanced, about one third of the way from the top or bottom of the frame is effective.

58 PHOTOGRAPHING SUNSETS

A sunset is a subject which few photographers can resist. Yet a surprisingly large percentage of sunset pictures are disappointing. There are a number of reasons why this should be so, since it can be a more difficult subject to capture on film successfully than it might at first seem.

The first mistake that many people make is to think that the sunset alone is sufficient to make an interesting picture. This is rarely the case and even when other elements such as foreground interest are included in the image, the exposure which will record the rich tones and colours in the sky will inevitably result in considerable loss of detail in these areas. One solution to this problem is to find some foreground interest which will be effective in silhouette, such as an interestingly-shaped tree for instance. Another technique is to choose a viewpoint which includes a reflective foreground, such as an expanse of water, to continue the tones of the sky. A third technique is to use a graduated filter to reduce the exposure in the sky area without affecting the foreground details. These can also be used to add colour to the sunset.

The calculation of exposure can also be a problem. One method which will give a satisfactory reading in most circumstances is to take a reading from the area of sky immediately above the camera. It is advisable to bracket exposures as the effect of the sunset will vary considerably according to the exposure and the best is difficult to predict.

Above Sunset in Death Valley. The soft, subtle colours were the result of shooting after the sun had gone down. A common mistake in sunset pictures is to take them too soon.

Right A 600mm lens was used to create this dramatic juxtaposition. Since no detail was needed in the silhouetted foreground figures, it was possible to select the best exposure for the sunset.

60 MULTIPLE EXPOSURES

Most cameras have a device which prevents the accidental exposure of two images on one piece of film. Such double exposure however can be used to create interesting and unusual pictures if done in a controlled way. You will either need a camera which enables two or more exposures to be made without advancing the film or to be prepared to wind the film back and re-expose it after having carefully marked the starting position.

The success of this technique lies in the juxtaposition and balance between the individual images and this requires that the final image is carefully planned. You must remember that as you are in effect reusing the film in the second and subsequent exposures that the lighter areas of one image must not be juxtaposed with light tones in the other. This will result in both being lost. The simplest way of ensuring success is to have one image basically dark in tone with the second image superimposed over it. To make it easier, you can underexpose the first or background image by as much as two stops or more. In most cases you will need to slightly underexpose the second image as well, as there is a cumulative effect and two or more normal exposures will produce an over-exposed final picture.

This type of picture is usually most successful when one image predominates and the other acts more as a background.

Right *The textured effect of this portrait was created by making an exposure of a piece of woven bamboo, lit to accentuate its texture, and then photographing the girl, who was placed against a black background, onto the same piece of film. The background shot was underexposed by two stops and the portrait by half a stop.*
Far right *Three separate exposures were used for this shot. The girl's profile was rim lit with a spotlight so that only a selective area was illuminated. The rest of the image is completely black, enabling three normal exposures to be made.*

Q What is the device that prevents double exposure?
A It is an internal mechanism which prevents the shutter from being released until the film is wound on.

Q How do you mark film for position for re-exposure?
A When you load the film, before closing the camera back and winding on to the first frame you must make a small mark on the film to line up with a precise point inside the camera, such as the edge of the film gate.

Q Can you make more than two exposures on one piece of film?
A Yes. You can make as many as you like, bearing in mind that the exposures will have a cumulative effect.

Q What is a slide duplicator?
A Basically it is a close-up device in which a slide is placed at the business end with a piece of Perspex behind it to diffuse the light. The inexpensive versions are used in place of a camera lens on an SLR.

In most cases a colour photograph is intended to give a fairly faithful record of the subject with perhaps a slight modification of the image to emphasize a particular quality or to create a more dramatic effect. There are, however, many ways in which the subject can be used only as a basis for the final image and the photographic process used as a means of changing and distorting it to create a more subjective and personally expressive image. Many of these techniques are relatively simple and can be done inside the camera, without recourse to the darkroom, simply by using and combining the characteristics of the film, lighting and filters. The following photographs demonstrate some of these effects.

Above *Infra-red Ektachrome was used for this surrealistic landscape. Its effect is not completely predictable, since it depends upon the invisible infra-red radiation. Kodak recommend the use of a starting point for experiments, but different filters and different exposures can produce a variety of effects. This shot was taken using a Cokin sepia filter with an exposure of 1/125 second at f8 in bright sunlight.*

Above right *This seascape was taken with the aid of an orange filter designed for use in black and white photography. Heavy filtration of this type can often be effective with the right subject. In this case, although the lighting was pleasing the unfiltered picture had a rather muddy, grey appearance and the filter added a degree of impact. This is an ideal way to use up stale or suspect film.*

Right *Soft focus is one of the simplest ways of creating a slightly different image quality. Used with the right subject, it is most effective. This shot was taken through strips of Sellotape (stretched) across the lenshood opening, leaving a clear spot in the centre. As well as the special attachments which can be bought as part of a filter system, there are many other ways of achieving this effect.*

Q I hear that some professionals use Vaseline on the filter for a soft focus technique. What is the effect?

A If it is smeared around the edges of a filter leaving a clear spot in the centre, it creates a soft focus effect combined with an attractive streaking of highlights. This can be controlled by teasing the jelly around with your fingertip. *Never* put Vaseline directly on the lens.

Above The strange colour quality of this still life shot was produced by illuminating the subject with ultraviolet light, sometimes called black light. In this case, sheets of fluorescent paper were illuminated by the ultraviolet lamp and reflected in a sheet of mirrored foil upon which the glasses were placed. This picture required an exposure of four seconds at f11 on ISO 200/24 daylight type film with a Kodak 2A UV filter to eliminate any scattered UV light.

Left The effect of this image was created by making three separate exposures – each through a tri-colour separation filter – red, green and blue, onto the same piece of film. Make an exposure through the red filter in the normal way. Without moving the camera or film, make an exposure through the green filter, giving one and a half stops extra, and another through the blue filter, giving two stops extra.

66 COLOUR AND BLUR

In most cases the camera settings are selected to create an image which is as sharp as possible. The shutter speed is fast enough to prevent camera or subject movement and the aperture small enough to ensure adequate depth of field. Yet the effect of blur can create quite powerful and attractive images in colour photography and you should consider the possibilities of using this quality as part of the composition when taking a picture.

Out of focus details can be created quite simply by using wide apertures and focussing the lens at a particular point of a subject and by framing the picture in such a way that objects much nearer and/or further are also included. This effect will be further emphasized by using long focus lenses.

Blur created by movement can be even more effective and can be achieved in a number of ways. With a subject that contains both a moving and a static element, such as a waterfall, the camera can be set up on a tripod and a slow shutter speed selected. This will record an image in which the static elements are sharp but the moving parts are blurred. With some subjects such as sports it is also possible to pan the camera with a moving subject and use a fairly slow shutter speed. This will produce an image in which the moving element is recorded sharply and the static part of the subject is blurred.

For those that like to experiment it can also be interesting to use a controlled camera shake combined with a slow shutter speed to introduce movement to a completely static subject.

Above *Controlled camera shake created effect. An exposure of 1/8 second was selected, the camera was wobbled carefully in a regular manner and the shutter released while it was moving.*
Left *For this shot the lens was adjusted so that it was completely out of focus. It was set at the closest focussing distance with the subject at infinity.*
Right *The slightly ghostly quality of this landscape picture was achieved by mounting the camera on a tripod and using a two-second exposure in poor light.*

68 MAKING A SLIDE SANDWICH

A slide sandwich is in effect the opposite of a double exposure, since the images are added together with dark tones building up against an essentially light background. There is the added advantage that you can also manipulate and judge the effect the images are creating as you do it.

Although eventually you will probably want to take shots specifically for an image you have visualized, to begin with it is a good idea to practise and experiment with slides you have already taken. It can be an economic way to use up not very successful slides. You will need a selection of rather overexposed slides, sorted into categories before you start. This type of picture, like the double exposure, works most effectively and easily when you have one image providing a fairly even background element, such as a pattern or a texture, and the other with a more boldly defined subject with a prominent shape or design. You could for instance have a silhouetted image of a tree sandwiched with, say, a picture of reflections in rippled water.

You will need some sort of light box or viewing screen so that the slides can be manipulated while you view the effect. When they are juxtaposed in the most effective way they can be taped together along one edge and fixed into a mount. In this form they can be shown in a projector or for a more permanent display.

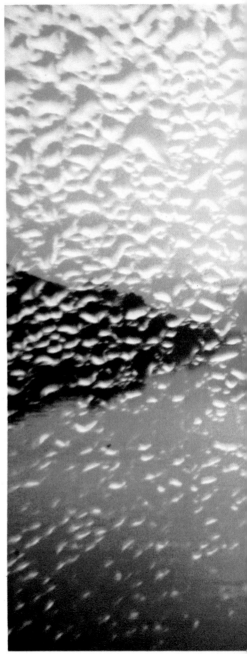

Above This sandwich was the result of combining two unsatisfactory pictures of the same scene to make one good one.
Right A transparency of a mountain reflected in a lake was contacted with a close-up picture of raindrops on a window.

70 PROCESSING COLOUR FILM

It is part of the natural progression from taking snapshots to making planned and satisfying photographs that you should not want to delegate the processing and printing of your pictures to some anonymous laboratory. Although processing colour film is largely a routine and mechanical procedure there is much satisfaction in being able to do it yourself, experiencing the almost magical transformation of a latent image into a full colour photograph.

All you will need in addition to the processing kit is a *developing tank*, a *photographic thermometer*, a selection of storage bottles and measures and a dark place to load the tank. Once the film is loaded into the tank the remaining steps can be carried out in daylight. As most colour processes are carried out at higher temperatures than that of the room being used, it is necessary to maintain the working temperatures of the solutions by immersing them (in their containers) in a large bowl of water heated to the correct temperature. Provided you follow the manufacturer's instructions carefully with regard to processing times and temperatures, and the film is agitated in the recommended way there is no reason why you should not obtain first class results every time. Make sure that you are scrupulously careful in the cleanliness of containers and utensils to avoid contamination.

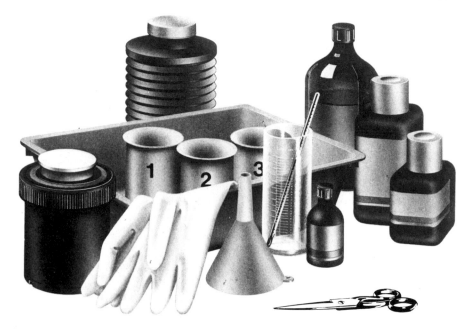

Above The items required for colour film processing – from left to right. A daylight developing tank, water bath, rubber gloves for mixing solutions, individual containers for each solution, a funnel, a measuring cylinder and thermometer, scissors, wetting agent, solution concentrates and, at the back, a concertina bottle for long-term storage.

Right The sequence for transferring a roll of exposed 35mm film, in darkness, after removing it from the cassette. From top to bottom. The film is aligned with the spiral held in one hand and the film, held by its edges, in the other. The leading edge is fed into the grooves of the spiral. Finally, twist the edges of the spiral back and forth until all the film is drawn in.

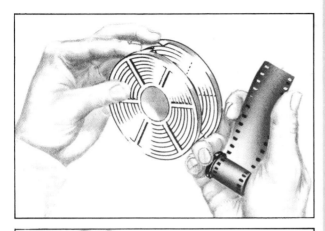

Q Is a darkroom feasible at home?

A Yes. It is a simple matter to set up a temporary darkroom – for even just a few hours – in any space that can be conveniently blacked out. A large cupboard will do. Running water is not essential. Many processes can be carried out in daylight once the film or paper is loaded into a light-tight tank. Essentially, any space that is large enough to accommodate you and the equipment you need and give you a little elbow room will make a perfectly adequate darkroom.

Q What will I need?

A For processing films you can even use a light-tight changing bag which can be bought in photographic stores, instead of a darkroom. You will also need a developing tank and film spiral, a measuring jug or cylinder, storage bottles for the solutions and an accurate photographic thermometer.

Q Do you treat negative film differently from transparency?

A The basic principle is the same, but the chemicals and sequence of processing is different.

Q What is the best way of drying film?

A The safest way to avoid damage and drying marks is to give the film a final rinse with wetting agent added to the water. Hang it up from a line in a dry, dust free place and let it dry naturally. For a quick dry you can use a squeegee to remove surplus water and place a fan heater in the room, but make sure that the squeegee blades are absolutely clean and that no drops of moisture are left behind on the film to cause drying marks.

Although colour transparencies can be viewed perfectly well by projection, you may also need to have prints made from them, either to give copies to friends or to use for display purposes. A print is in any case a very satisfying way of viewing a photograph and to make your own allows you to realize the full potential of the picture. Making prints from transparencies is in many ways easier than from colour negatives, particularly for beginners.

In addition to the equipment required for black and white printing, and of course the colour paper and chemicals, you will also need a set of *colour printing filters* or an enlarger with a *colour head*. Since it is somewhat more difficult to process colour paper than black and white in open dishes, a *print processing drum* is also recommended. Once loaded in darkness the remaining steps can be carried out in room light. The prepared solutions can be brought to the recommended working temperature and maintained in the same sort of water bath used for processing film. In addition to establishing the correct exposure for the print by means of test strips you will also have to find the correct colour balance and adjust it by the use of the colour printing filters.

Remember that when printing from transparencies, more exposure produces a lighter print and you need a filter of the opposite colour to correct a colour cast – for example a red filter to correct a cyan cast.

***Right** The effect of giving both more and less than the correct exposure. The exposure latitude of a reversal paper such as Cibachrome is greater than that of negative/positive papers and up to 20 per cent variation will seldom be critical. Because of reciprocity failure, however, it is better to make major changes in the exposure by varying the aperture of the enlarging lens rather than the exposure time. Do not forget to make an allowance in the exposure when adding or subtracting filters.*

Q What is an enlarger with a colour head?
A It is an enlarger with a light source that can be controlled by dials to alter its colour quality. An ordinary enlarger with a set of colour printing filters will do just as well.

Q How do you make a test strip?
A You place a strip of the paper you will use for the finished print – about one-third of a sheet – in the most important part of the picture area and give it a basic exposure, say about five seconds. Cover about a fifth of it with a piece of opaque material and repeat the action five times. If it is all too light or too dark, repeat the test increasing or decreasing the basic exposure accordingly. When you find the most satisfactory exposure, note it down.

Above An exposed colour print being loaded into a processing drum. The print is curled with the emulsion on the inside and then fed into the drum. The room light can be switched on when the lid is in place, and the processing solutions can be poured through the light-tight hole.

Below A water bath or tempering unit. This allows the maintenance of an accurately controlled temperature. A small quantity of each solution is poured into the drum in sequence, which is then replaced in the water bath and rotated either by hand or by an electric motor.

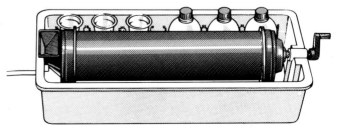

The basic equipment required is the same as for printing from transparencies – an enlarger with a colour head or a set of colour printing filters and a print processing drum. The exposure and colour balance assessment is, however, quite different. You will need to make one or more test strips to establish these factors and they both tend to be more critical than for reversal prints. Remember that greater exposure will produce a darker print when printing from a colour negative and that to correct a colour cast you must use a correction filter of the same colour as the cast – a blue filter to correct a blue cast and so forth. Unlike reversal printing you will find that quite small variations in filtration and exposure will make a significant difference to the print quality, so it is necessary to make test strips and filtration changes in quite small increments.

It is a good idea before embarking on making enlargements to make a set of contact prints. This will not only make it easier to choose the best negatives but will also help you to assess the differences in exposure and filtration that will be needed for different negatives. It is also a good idea to have a standard negative, one which contains a full range of tones and colours including grey, and to make a good print from it, noting the exact details of filtration and exposure. Then if you experience problems or change to a different paper you can refer back to your standard negative to help identify the error or establish what changes are needed.

Above and right With colour printing, exposure and colour filtration have to be controlled. Select a filter of the same colour as the colour bias in order to eliminate it – a print which is too blue will need a blue filter. Allow for the addition or subtraction of filters by adjusting the exposure time. Each batch of paper has a recommended filter pack, which should be used for the first test to establish the correct exposure. The next tests should attempt to correct any colour bias in the first by adjusting the filter pack. The illustrations compare red, green, blue, cyan, magenta and yellow colour bias with the correct print. **Left** A Kodak Ektaflex colour printer.

76 IDENTIFYING FAULTS

Everybody, including the most experienced photographers, makes mistakes and occasionally gets disappointing results. Unfortunately the inexperienced photographer often finds it difficult to identify the cause of the error since even the most basic fault, such as the image being too dark, can be caused by a number of different factors. The following examples are intended to help you discover the exact reason for a failure and to indicate how to avoid it in the future.

Below An unsharp image can be caused in a variety of ways. If, as in this picture, part of the image is sharp but the rest unsharp, it may be the result of the shutter speed not being fast enough to freeze a moving element in the scene. It can also be caused by inaccurate focussing or by not using a small enough aperture to obtain adequate depth of field.

Right A pale image with washed-out colours is most commonly the result of overexposure, setting the film speed to an ISO number lower than that of the film in use or by allowing the meter to be influenced by abnormally large dark tones.
Below right A dark, murky image is invariably the result of underexposure. Setting the camera or exposure meter to a film speed faster than that of the film being used is the first thing to check. Failing to make any allowance for a filter when using non-TTL metering can also easily be done.

One area of photography which is often neglected by otherwise careful workers is presentation of their photographs. This is a pity, since good presentation will not only greatly enhance even the best pictures but it will also prevent them from deteriorating.

It is important to remember that all photographic materials will be damaged unless they are stored away from extreme temperatures, damp and humidity and are kept in darkness when not being displayed. Colour transparencies should be mounted and protected in acetate sleeves. These can be in the form of viewpacks, which make for easy access and filing, or in the more elaborate card mounts, which also provide an effective means of presentation with more room for identification. Colour prints should be mounted for maximum protection and the surface should also be covered. Small prints can be mounted several to a page into an album with acetate covered leaves. If the pictures are carefully selected and laid out to create a pleasingly balanced arrangement this in itself is an impressive form of display. Larger prints can be dry mounted onto mounting boards and either stored in a portfolio box or a portfolio album with acetate sleeves. Extra finish and protection can be given by the use of cutout overlays or mats.

Your very best pictures can make an effective contribution to the decor of your home or office when framed, but remember to hang them well away from direct sunlight. If possible use the Cibachrome process for your prints as this is more resistant to fading.

Right Good photographs can make an effective contribution to the decor of a room if they are chosen well and mounted and framed to complement each other. While a single strong image can often stand well on its own, it can often be more interesting to plan and arrange a group of pictures in the way shown in this illustration.

Q Are there ways of mounting photographs other than by dry mounting?

A Yes, you can use a rubber adhesive such as cow gum or an aerosol spray mountant, but you should ensure that what you use is recommended for photographs as some adhesives contain chemicals that could cause the prints to stain or discolour.

Q Is there any way of protecting colour prints from fading when displayed?

A Some additional protection may be gained by the use of a UV absorbing glass, or spray, which can be obtained from dealers.

Q How can you clean sticky fingermarks from slides and prints?

A Special fluid is obtainable from photographic stores, but you can use carbon tetrachloride.

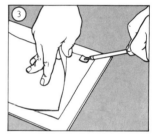

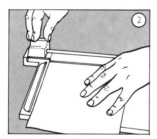

Above The stages involved in dry mounting. 1 The adhesive tissue is positioned on the back of the print and fixed at the centre with a hot tacking iron. 2 The print is trimmed flush with the tissue. 3 The print and attached tissue are positioned on the card mount and the corners are tacked down with the iron. 4 The print and mount are then slid into the heated press with a protective sheet on each side. 5 Pressure is applied for the recommended time.

80 INDEX